THE WHITE MOUNTAINS
of New Hampshire

Photographs and Text by Alan Nyiri

Down East Books
Camden, Maine

Friendship is the yardstick with which I measure my wealth. Immeasurable thanks go to Angele, Daniel, Ellen, Nancy and Gary, and Polly and Ernie for making my life so rich.

Special thanks need to be given to Ken Rancourt, Director Guy Gosselin, and all the members of the Mount Washington Observatory for their cooperation and assistance with this project.

Design and layout by Alan Nyiri
Composition and printing by Argentofot, W. Germany

5 4 3 2 1

Down East Books / Camden, Maine

Contents

Steep Trails and High Places

I'm standing on the summit of Mount Washington on the rarest of days. The winds are only five to seven miles per hour — barely enough to push the anemometer cups around. Visibility is as good as it ever gets; mountains in New York State, 130 miles distant, can be seen. In the forest below the autumn color is at its peak, but takes on a pastel palette because of the distance. While the Mount Washington Observatory staff confirms the rarity of these conditions to the crowd of visitors, I just try to admire, enjoy, and utilize my good fortune.

This late-September morning dawned very cold and very clear, not unusual for the White Mountains in New Hampshire. What *was* unusual was the absolute absence of air movement, both in my valley location and in the peaks area. Now a small wisp of cloud — the only one visible to me — hangs unmoving over Mount Adams, and even that slowly begins to dissipate as I watch. Clear, still air is an anomaly in these mountains. The summit of Mount Washington sits in the clouds over 300 days each year; windless days can be counted on the toes of a snake. For me, this rare combination of favorable conditions means I can use my 4x5 view camera at the summit, an opportunity not to be missed. Without hesitation I load up for a day's hike and set out for the base station of the Cog Railroad.

Sure, I'm cheating. Let the cute little train carry me up the mountain, and then enjoy a lazy stroll down. But I'm not out today to make a macho statement; I'm looking to create photographic images. Besides, I know about these lazy strolls down mountains . . .!

At the summit, I unload my view camera and begin work. Every way I turn, images compete for the attention of eye and lens. But I can't shoot here all afternoon, or use all my film; I must save time and film for the hike back down the Ammonoosuc Ravine Trail.

As the highest mountain in New England — in fact, the entire Northeast — Mount Washington offers a view that can only be called spectacular. On a clear day such as today, row after row of gentle hills and mountains can be seen receding into the blue distance. To the north, the hills of Quebec are visible. The Green Mountains of Vermont can be seen to the west, and beyond them the Adirondacks in New York. The view to the south scans over the southern White Mountains to the lake region of New Hampshire and into the Berkshires of Massachusetts. To the southeast, I look over the hills of Maine and see a brilliant flash along the horizon — the sun reflecting off the Atlantic Ocean, a most amazing sight to me. The Camden Hills of mid-coast Maine are perceivable to the east, while the Rangeley Lakes of northwestern Maine can be seen to the northeast.

Normally I wouldn't undertake a hike like this until my legs had had a week's conditioning. But although I'd arrived here in the mountains for my autumn shoot only three days ago, the conditions are perfect today, so this hike can "speed condition" me for the others to follow. Hefting the fifty-five-pound view camera pack into the grooves worn into my shoulders, I set off down the mountain.

The first leg of my journey, the Crawford Path, descends about 1200 feet to the Lakes of the Clouds. Although a number of people are out on the trail today, this is a good opportunity

Looking west through New Hampshire, Vermont, and New York.

to collect my thoughts and impressions away from the much larger crowd that has gathered on the summit. While most folks have driven up the Mount Washington Auto Road or have taken the Cog Railroad as I did, a few hardy hikers pass me on their way to the top. This trail, about 1.4 miles long, is entirely above timberline. People have described this landscape as being almost lunar; indeed, the entire summit region is littered with a jumble of mica schist scree, giving you a first impression that nothing exists up here but bare rock. Actually, life abounds among the broken glacial talus. Approximately 110 high-elevation plant species grow in this alpine zone, most isolated on these higher mountain slopes. Wherever soil has had a chance to collect – even in the tiniest cracks between rocks – plants move in to colonize. Lichens, mosses, grasses, sedges, and numerous alpine flowers occupy these spaces. Many are so diminutive that they are barely noticeable, and are thus overlocked by the casual viewer.

Above treeline only a few animals foray. Several species of mice and shrews live up here, and some species of songbirds come up to feed in good weather. Hawks and ravens are common, and almost one hundred species of insects can be found. While the large species found most frequently on the high peaks is man, Greg Gordon of the Mount Washington Observatory staff has a wonderful picture of a full-racked moose wandering around the mountain slopes. I hesitate to even speculate what the moose could have been looking for, unless he just came up for the view!

The hike down the Crawford Path is exhilarating! Although the trail is somewhat rough and loose rock seems determined to make me lose my footing, the incredible vistas overpower these perils of hiking. With several short photographic "rest" stops, I arrive at the Lakes of the Clouds area around 2 p.m. The first hardy trees appear here: low-growing, dense mats of balsam fir and black spruce called *krummholz*. This growing adaptation provides protection from the arctic conditions to these small, dwarf forests; in winter, the snow trapped by the krummholz provides cover against the shearing gales. The lakes themselves – actually small ponds – are still and unrippled in the windless air, and beckon me to explore and photograph. I give them two hours, more time than I really have, and reluctantly push on.

Leaving the Crawford Path by the famed Lakes of the Clouds Appalachian Mountain Club Hut, I swing onto the Ammonoosuc Ravine Trail. Immediately the trail begins to descend sharply through a scrub forest of dwarf black spruce, balsam fir, birch, and alpine willow. Birds of the far Canadian north woods find this habitat to their liking; blackpoll warblers and gray-cheeked thrushes flit through the spruce branches. The ubiquitous whitethroated sparrow sings his bittersweet song, so perfect in these lonely mountain heights. Steep rock slabs, still wet with the runoff of recent rains, challenge my footing, in some places forcing me to use the "three-point, wet-butt" sliding technique. In some places these slabs drop fifteen or twenty feet, without footholds, handholds, or breakfalls.

I hear myself exclaiming, "They expect me to slide down that? What do I look like – a mountain goat?"

The view south from Wildcat Mountain.

Mumbling and grumbling, I descend quickly down the steep trail into the ever-taller boreal forest, crisscrossing numerous streams and rivulets. At last I am rewarded for my efforts: standing on a ledge in the middle of a shallow stream, I have a wonderful view of the western mountains as the afternoon ripens into evening. Indeed, I am running out of day, and still have several mountain miles to travel.

The trail here changes from steep rock slabs to steep rock "stairs." Trail crews have built these to slow erosion. (Trail crews, I might add, consisting of men seven feet and taller, if the height of these stairs is any indication.) For a person of average height, hopping from one rock to the next is the only means of descent. And for a person not conditioned to mountain hiking, this form of descent takes a heavy toll on one's legs. I sure am glad when the roar of a waterfall "forces" me to take a photo break.

Around me, the forest is changing too. I've descended into the predominant transition forest, where hardwoods begin to appear in the spruce-fir zone. The lower I go, the more mountain ash, beech, sugar maple, and yellow birch I'll encounter. However, I'm sorry to say that inner changes are distracting me from the changes taking place around me. The pounding of the last mile's descent has left my legs like rubber. The long shadows and golden glow remind me that I don't have long before darkness sets in, and my legs are not at all sure they want to carry me the rest of the way, regardless of how much daylight remains. I have to literally force myself to stop to make several images, torn between the need to work with the lovely evening light (and give myself a much-needed rest at the same time), and the fear of being stranded on the trail after dark. Happily, my images are made, and I still manage to stagger back to the base station of the Cog Railroad just in time for a wonderful sunset.

While I splurge on a sumptuous feast at the Cog Railroad Restaurant – my reward to myself for a good day's work – I have time to reflect on the unique experience of the outing. Over the course of the afternoon, I've traveled the equivalent of a thousand-mile trip. I started in a climatological region similar to the tundra of Labrador, and "hiked" 100 miles south with each 400 feet I descended, sampling many diverse life zones. I've had a chance to experience the vast variety of flora and fauna for which the White Mountains are fabled and to make many unique and rewarding images. And finally, I've been blessed with the opportunity to enjoy Mount Washington in one of her rarest and most benevolent moods, for this is a mountain that thinks nothing of knocking down her visitors with hundred-mile-per-hour winds and freezing them in sudden summertime snowstorms. This is a mountain that can kill!

Mount Adams from the northeast flank of Mount Washington.

Krummholz nestles among the rocks along the (almost) mile-high Lakes of the Clouds.

The summit of Middle Sugerloaf affords wonderful views in all directions. Below, the smooth, polished surface of the western slope attests to the grinding action of the last glacier. At right, just yards away on the east slope, glacial plucking has carried off huge blocks of stone, creating cliffs.

The transition forest on the eastern slopes of Crawford Notch (above) shows the diversity of trees growing in this type of environment. A canopy of maples, beech, and yellow birch creates the wonderful yellow glow of this mixed hardwood forest (left).

An easy climb to Mount Willard rewards the hiker with these spectacular vistas of Crawford Notch.

Ledges along the Swift River further demonstrate the rich diversity of the transition forest (left). Above, spruce gain a foothold in the birch forest along the path to Mount Willard.

On a brilliant autumn afternoon, the setting sun spotlights Eagle Cliff in Franconia Notch. Mount Lafayette and Echo Lake can also be seen in this view from Bald Mountain (below). At right, the slopes of Cannon Mountain (seen from Profile Lake) form the steepest and narrowest section of the notch.

These images are more about different qualities of light than about trees. High overcast conditions created the soft, diffuse light so perfect for photographing this forest of birch, maple, beech, and spruce (left). The first rays of the sun seem to ignite the foliage of a suger maple (above).

The jumbled chaos of the mica-schist boulders covering the summit of Mount Washington is evident in the photo below. At right, Mount Washington stands capped with rime ice against a flawless December sky.

The Roar of the Mountain

Jasper, the yellow tabby, sleeps peacefully under the stove where I've been baking chocolate chip cookies. Inga, Jasper's calico partner in feline crimes, jumps down from the carpeted play tree where she's been sharpening her claws, and affectionately rubs up against my boots. She's ready to go out – well, not *out,* but out to the unheated portion of the building. I start to dress, for I am going *out.* First, I slip on two pairs of wool socks and a cotton turtleneck. Then follows a layer of thermal underwear covered by heavy wool pants and an equally heavy wool shirt. I next don a thick wool sweater an felt-pac boots. Now I'm ready to go out to the anteroom with Inga and finish dressing. Glasses, goggles, camera lens, and viewer eyepiece first get an anti-fog coating. Then I don outerwear: wool headpiece, face-mask, and balaclava complete my headgear, an expedition-weight down parka and nylon ski-pants protect my body, and crampons attached to my boots secure my footing. Finally, I pull on silk glove liners, followed by heat-reflective synthetic liners, and over all, a snow-mobile mitten for my left hand and a more manageable down glove for my shutter-finger hand. Now I'm ready to go **out!**

The Mount Washington Observatory crouches at the summit of the 6288-foot peak – highest in the Northeast. Established in 1932 to conduct meteorological observations and scientific research, the observatory is run by a nonprofit, private corporation that today occupies part of the Sherman Adams Summit Building. I've come up for a week in mid-December to sample the weather and create whatever images conditions will allow. After several days of being fogged-in (the most common weather condition), a high-pressure system and cold front have cleared the summit for at least a few hours. I can hear the roar of the northwest wind from the weather room as I make one last check of the outside conditions before entering the airlock of the observatory tower.

Although the weather today is not at all unusual for the summit in December, it is a bit rugged. The wind has picked up from when I started dressing, and is now blowing between ninety and a hundred miles per hour, with gusts to 120. The temperature at noon is still minus twelve degrees Fahrenheit, about what it's been since midnight. Under these conditions wind-chill factors have little meaning, and are practically incalculable anyway. The wind-chill table in the weather room extends to "only" fifty miles per hour, and even then indicates a factor of 76 degrees below zero at this temperature. At 100 miles per hour and twelve below, I don't want to know… it doesn't matter! Any exposed skin freezes in seconds, and frostbite danger is extremely high even when properly clothed.

Trusting that I'm adequately dressed, I step out of the weather tower airlock onto the roof. The wind hits me full blast, sucking the air out of my lungs and threatening to knock me over. At this velocity a gust could easily sweep me off my feet, even though I'm wearing crampons, and blow me across the roof. The danger is not so great here – the railing surrounding the roof would catch me – but where I'm headed, there is little protection from being literally blown off the mountain. If knocked down away from the summit buildings,

An observatory staff member disappears into the fog during "white-out" conditions (above). Winds exceeding 100 miles per hour whip cloud fragments and blowing snow into the frenzy pictured below.

I could only hope to dig in with my ice axe and crampons to keep from being tumbled and blown across the treeless, ice-covered summit.

I decide to practice walking for a while where it's relatively safe, on the roof and between buildings. No method is easy; you can only lean into the wind and use your ice axe for support. Moving into the wind is both the most difficult and the safest. While you are least likely to be swept off your feet when leaning into it, at times the wind completely stops you from moving ahead and is as impossible to push into as pushing through a brick wall. Moving across the wind calls for tricky balance and a delicate sensitivity to sudden changes in wind direction and force – but moving *with* the wind can be really terrifying! You are constantly fighting a force that would soon have you flying across the terrain, attempting to match the wind's velocity. I find that the best plan is to stand leaning into the wind during the worst gusts, and move only during comparative lulls.

After I've moved around for a while and feel somewhat confident of my ability to negotiate in this wind, I start to explore the summit. I've become well-enough accustomed to the physical banging and beating to become aware of wind's other realities. Most demanding on my senses is its roar. Yet as I seek shelter in the lee of the transmitter building to better observe and listen, I realize that this roar is really an amalgamation of many separate sounds. Each object the wind rushes by vibrates at its own frequency; each rock, each antenna, each guy wire shrieks with its own special sound. Acting as coordinator for this cacophony is the air itself. At this velocity even the air vibrates, as molecules of oxygen and nitrogen slam into the mountain and everything on it. I can't help but wonder how the mountain roared on April 12, 1934, when the highest winds ever recorded blew across Mount Washington. If 120-mile-per-hour winds are practically deafening me now, whatever could the sound of a 231-mile-per-hour gale have been?

Oddly, my visual sensitivities are the last to come fully alive today. Perhaps my brain has determined that other senses require priority in this situation. My instincts may have noted that sense of balance and audible early warning of dangerous gusts would be the senses most required for survival. But now, seated in shelter from most of the wind, I begin to concentrate on the visual spectacle around me. Covering the ground and every object on it (from the 4500-foot level) is a thick layer of rime ice. As supercooled droplets of fog strike the high summit regions they freeze on impact, creating impossibly delicate feathers of ice on every object. These formations grow into the wind, sometimes at a rate of several inches per hour, and can achieve a length of two or more feet. Strong enough to withstand 200-mile-per-hour winds, nonetheless the rime crumbles to the touch, sounding like brittle styrofoam.

Other than the fanciful formations of rime, the most striking visual feature of this unusual world is the passing of the clouds. Actually, they don't just pass … they streak past and over the summit at over a hundred miles per hour, creating the illusion of flying through them in a plane. Mixed with the clouds is any loose snow or ice picked up from the lower slopes; the incessant winds allow very little snow accumulation at this altitude. The sky can be perfectly

A new coat of rime ice begins to coat the Stage Office on Mount Washington's summit.

clear one moment, and the next a cloud boils up the western slope to obliterate the sun, sky, and even nearby buildings. I find a great challenge in attempting to capture in photographs the eerie emotions that sweep over me as the clouds pass over the summit.

After three days of being enclosed by fog, here on the summit, I'm anxious to make some images now that it has finally cleared. My original intention for today was to move down to the eastern icefield on the lee side of the mountain to do some photography, and since the cold and wind seem manageable, I decide to proceed with this plan. But first, I will return to the observatory and check the forecast for the afternoon, have a quick cup of coffee, and inform the crew of my intended destination.

Leaving the protection of the transmitter building, I cover about half the distance back to the observatory when a violent gust of wind (later confirmed at 130 miles per hour) sweeps me off my feet and blows me about ten yards across the ice. Caught unaware, I have difficulty digging in with my ice axe, but the Cog Railroad tracks offer a foothold, allowing me to stop myself. After sitting there until I decide I'm not going into cardiac arrest after all, I return inside to rethink my plans.

On March 24, 1983, two hikers climbed up from Tuckerman's Ravine on a day very much like today. Heading north down the carriage road near the parking lots, they were assailed by winds as they left the summit, and decided that by moving just below the track of the road on the eastern slope they might gain some protection. Unfortunately, this didn't help. A gust knocked them both off their feet and sent them tumbling hundreds of yards down the steep, boulder-strewn slope. Only one of them survived. Three days later, a hiker on the Tuckerman's Ravine Trail met with a similar fate.

As I remove the layers of clothing, back inside, I also think about the experience of photographer Dean Brown. In the summer of 1973, while photographing on Table Mountain, Dean sustained fatal injuries when he fell while traversing a slippery moss-covered ledge. His last photograph appears in the Time-Life book *New England Wilds*. While I want very much to make some images of the extraordinary scene outside, I certainly don't wish to duplicate the experience of Mr. Brown. I have the proper clothing and equipment, but I'd be breaking a prime rule of wilderness hiking in extreme conditions: *never hike alone.* So now, while sipping a cup of hot coffee in the weather room, I decide that discretion truly is the better part of valor. I'll pack away my camera gear for the rest of the day and write for a while instead. There will be other opportunities to photograph the roar of the mountain.

The col between Mount Clay and Mount Washington.

This photograph of the Weather Observatory tower started as a moonset shot, but clouds moved in during the final minutes, leaving only a sliver of sky on the horizon for the sunrise to peek through (above). This was the only sun we'd see this day. With two cameras set up in sheltered positions, I was able to catch these moments of alpenglow.

When fog covers the summit, the droplets of water freeze on contact with every object, coating it with rime ice. At the summit of Mount Washington (left), the rock-strewn ground is building up an ever-thicker coating of rime. Down at around 4000 feet (above), a thin layer of rime on tree branches indicates the lower reach of the recent fog cover.

Mount Clay from across the windswept Cow Pasture. On my last day on the mountain the weather cleared and the wind dropped to almost nothing, enabling me to hike down the mountain to get these images.

Still, it was a tough decision: hike down and photograph, or let the Sno-cat bring my gear down and descend the way the crew often does at shift-change, by sled! Imagine: an eight-mile, 4000-foot vertical drop sled ride. I'll have to go back to experience that! Below, I'm looking across Huntington Ravine towards Tuckerman Ravine.

Around midnight on the night of the full moon, the clouds cleared and winds dropped to only 25 to 30 miles per hour. I've always wanted to photograph a moonlit snow scene, and this view of the TV station from the entrance of the Sherman Adams Summit Building provided a fine subject.

Alpenglow on Mount Madison.

Falling Waters and Rising Mists

All right! I'll admit it . . . I love waterfalls. So much so, in fact, that when I came up to New Hampshire in July to start this book project, I spent almost the entire first two weeks following streams that led to waterfalls, trying to visit at least the major ones. Even then I only scratched the surface, for there are hundreds and hundreds of waterfalls throughout the White Mountains.

Actually, it's not just the falls themselves that attract me, nor the sales potential of whatever images I might make of them (waterfalls being a popular subject). I'm drawn to moving water in general, whether it's a gently babbling brook flowing through a quiet valley, or a mighty cataract tumbling hundreds of feet over a steep cliff. And I'm fascinated by the environments that brooks, streams, and falls create. The energy of falling water, capable of tearing down mountains and carving deep canyons, excites me and brings me alive, no matter what the scale. It imparts this energy to all the life sharing its surroundings as well. Plants are almost always more abundant along a stream's course, and animals are drawn to the water for physical sustenance just as I am for spiritual nourishment. Thus, it's not at all strange that as soon as I arrived in the mountains, I immediateley headed for water.

Fortunately for waterfall addicts, many of the White Mountain's most beautiful falls are readily accessible. A particularly interesting falls lies at the head of one of this area's most famous geologic features: the Flume. This is a narrow gorge only twelve to twenty feet wide with sheer granite walls rising seventy to ninety feet, formed by the erosion of a relatively soft basaltic dike in 200-million-year-old Conway granite. The 800-foot-long gorge is lined by a boardwalk that allows visitors to walk between the perpendicular walls. Along the boardwalk you can observe the lush ferns, mosses, and wildflowers that grow in the cracks as you travel to the head of the gorge. Here Flume Brook roars over Avalanche Falls, a forty-five-foot drop into the Flume.

You may notice that I rarely include the entire falls in my pictures. I try instead to find the "heart" of the falls, the part that is most characteristic of its spirit or contains the falls' peak energy.

Near the Flume is another area of high interest for me. The Pemigewasset River has carved a large basin – logically enough called the Basin – in the granite near the entrance of Cascade Brook. Centuries of erosion have transformed the hard granite into sensuous, fluid lines that excite the imagination. A short hike up Cascade Brook is also quite rewarding; in addition to following the brook up across wide, smooth ledges (perfect for sunning in hot weather), the trail leads past Kinsman and Rocky Glen falls, two delightful cascades.

A few miles to the north, near Franconia Notch, is a trail any serious waterfall-watcher should explore. Appropriately named the Falling Waters Trail, it runs along Walker Brook and past the lovely Walker Cascade for a short distance, then crosses over to Dry Brook and continues beside it. During the moderate climb up Dry Brook you pass Stairs Falls, Swiftwater Falls, and my favorite, Cloudland Falls, a graceful eighty-foot stepped cascade lying just below two smaller falls.

If I were to pinpoint all the falls I've visited, this book would have to be three times longer, but I do have to mention a few more worth seeking out: particularly noteworthy are Bridal

Lower Falls on the Swift River.

41

Veil Falls near Easton; Champney Falls off the Kancamagus Highway, near Conway; Crystal Cascade near the Pinkham Notch AMC Hut; Glen Ellis Falls in Pinkham Notch; Nancy Cascade on the Nancy Brook Trail; Ripley Falls on the Ethan Pond Trail; Sabbaday Falls off the Kancamagus Highway; and Zealand Falls, next to the AMC Hut of the same name. And I shouldn't overlook New Hampshire's highest waterfall, 200-foot Arethusa Falls, just south of the Willey House site in Crawford Notch. Excellent views of this cascade make it a photographer's delight.

One can invert the old saying and state that everything that comes down must go back up again. This is certainly true of water; in nature all water eventually evaporates, condensing into clouds to fall once again as rain, continuing the neverending cycle. Usually this is a quiet, unseen operation, but one morning I had the opportunity to watch the evaporation process, in a show I'll never forget.

It had rained all night, a cold, dreary, October kind of rain — a little bit colder and it would have been snow. Before dawn, I could see that the sky was beginning to clear, so I drove up the Kancamagus Highway in search of a place to view the sunrise. I stopped at the Sugar Hill Overlook about thirty minutes before sunrise; it seemed like the perfect place. It was peaceful and quiet, and I was alone. Well sure enough, just as the morning light-show was about to begin, another vehicle pulled up and a pile of cameras got out. I must admit that I rather resented having my solitude broken, but the other photographer certainly had as much right to be there as I did. Still, since I had just recently captured a magnificent sunrise elsewhere, and since I didn't see any foreground subject here that appealed to me anyway, I didn't bother to get out my camera gear. Let the other guy shoot away; for once I intended to relax and just enjoy the show.

But then the magic happened! The sun broke over the horizon, and within minutes began to warm the billions of dewdrops clinging to every leaf and twig. As the dew began to evaporate, mists rose from the forest below us, and layers of fog started to form. By this time I was squirming with enthusiasm and ran to my truck to get my 4x5 camera. Working quickly with the rapidly evolving drama before us, the other dawn photographer and I exchanged knowing, excited glances from time to time, but did not speak lest we break the spell that enveloped us. At last the sun rose higher, the mists and fogs evaporated for good, and it was over. When we met at our vehicles, I exclaimed, "That was *incredible!*"

"I've never seen anything *like* it" he agreed, speaking with a distinctive German accent. We ended up chatting for an hour, and I learned that he was indeed a German photographer, working on a book about New England for a British publisher. When we ran into each other again the next day we found it amusing, and good-natured charges of photographic espionage were exchanged. But when a week later we ran into each other in a photo shop near Harvard University, the coincidence seemed too great. Over lunch, we compared images and discussed our respective book projects, occasionally chuckling again over the situation. We felt a part of the rain/evaporation cycle we had recently witnessed, the way we were appearing and disappearing from each other's lives.

I wish you and *your* book success, Kirt.

The magic begins …

The base of Stairs Falls on the Falling Waters Trail, spotlighted as the sun just peeks out of the clouds (left). Above, the head of Avalanche Falls as it plummets into the Flume.

The form and shape of falling water (right) repeats itself in the granite it leaves behind at the Basin (below).

Water-rounded boulders along the Swift River shine after a shower (above). Thousands of spring floods have worn down these once-angular blocks of granite. A side stream into Cascade Brook performs a similar operation on a much smaller scale (left).

Cloudland Falls: my reward for hiking up the Falling Waters Trail. As I looked over the area, these two images presented themselves to me as a pair, a rather unusual occurrence.

Although all my photographs are essentially more about light than about subject, the quality of light in these images particularly reinforces this idea. At left, early morning sun creates a tranquil mood along the Ammonoosuc River. Above, the cool blue light of dawn gives these birches by the Pemigewasset River an almost metallic quality.

Below and right: Arethusa Falls, queen of New Hampshire's waterfalls. Cascading over 200 feet, it is the highest in the state.

Oxalis carpets a glen along Dry Brook (above), while a recent shower brings a glow to the foliage along the Saco River (right).

The Glen Ellis Falls in winter presents a totally different facade from the view most people see (left). Downriver, a fresh snow capping the exposed boulders creates temporary islands.

Fog shrouds the Nancy Cascade on Nancy Brook (left). Above, the sudden evaporation of billions of dewdrops creates swirling mists and fog.

Mists condense into more substantial clouds, creating a magical cloudscape.

Warm, moist, valley air rises to the much cooler heights of the Presidential Range and condenses into the cloud cover so common over the peaks throughout the year.

Reflections and Other Pondicherrian Delights

A pink blush begins to illuminate the eastern sky on this early October morning. It's 5:45 and I'm hidden in the bushes along Cherry Pond. I've been coming here each morning for several days now, hoping to photograph the moose that populate this area. Cherry Pond and its smaller companion, Little Cherry Pond, are the heart of the 305-acre Pondicherry Wildlife Refuge, an Audubon Sanctuary in the western foothills of the White Mountains. This remote, unspoiled valley provides a diversity of woodland, pond, and open-heath bog habitats that attract most of the animals and birdlife associated with northern New England. Fresh tracks indicate that moose come here frequently, probably to feed.

Although I'm not a wildlife photographer, I feel a strong need to photograph a moose in its environment for this book project. For me, the moose is the quintessential symbol of the northern woods, and until I've photographed one on his own turf, I won't feel that I've fully experienced the essence of these mountains.

The blush in the eastern sky has increased to a glow, and I am beginning to see my surroundings in some detail. From my vantage point on the western edge of the pond, I can see approximately sixty acres of open heath mat bordering the ninety-acre pond. A bog forest of black spruce and larch lies beyond, the larches (or tamarack) now a brilliant yellow as they prepare to shed their needles. In the distance, the western slopes of the Presidential Range rise out of the mists, silhouetted against the sunrise.

The weather front moving in from the west has brought in low cumulus clouds, gliding toward the eastern horizon at just the right altitude and time. It appears that I may be in store for an unexpected treat.

I watch more intently from my place of hidden silence for signs of a moose coming to feed. The sky brightens and begins to deepen in color, while the gentlest of breezes faintly stirs the water and tickles the spike rushes growing in the shallows. Now the clouds begin to assume dramatic forms and colors, and I find I'm rapidly loosing my interest in moose. Above me, one of the most spectacular sunrises I've ever witnessed is taking place. Could I be so lucky as to have a moose wander out of the brush into this perfect sunrise, too?

The now-violent hues above are in sharp contrast to the pervasive stillness surrounding me. Mists rise silently off the pond, while around me the autumn foliage appears to ignite with the reflected red light from the sky. The piercing cry of a loon from somewhere across the lake suddenly shatters the silence, startling me. Somewhere, too, a moose standing knee-deep in water, munching a breakfast of aquatic plants, may be startled by the cry of another loon. Somewhere . . . but not here.

This morning I wait in vain for my moose; none will show. Yet I can't say I'm disappointed, for I've just had the opportunity to witness and photograph a most glorious and satisfying sunrise. As I watch, the dawn evolves into a panorama of swirling clouds and rising mists,

Sorry, no moose . . .

but the show's not over yet! The mirrorlike surface of Cherry Pond seems to take on a life of its own, and I find all thoughts of moose evaporate with the mists as my imagination is captivated by the ever-changing reflections. I've come out hunting for moose, but find myself caught instead by clouds and reflections.

I've just recently started to concentrate on photographing reflections, and the events of this early morning steer me in this direction. Driving to the Ammonoosuc River, where still, deep pools and broad ledges of wet granite will be a perfect hunting ground for this type of image, I can't help but "reflect" on this new focus of my work. For years I've noticed that the focus of my images parallels the direction of my personal growth. When I was learning to deal with major changes in my personal life, my images were obviously about relationships. While learning to cope with the changes that long work trips necessitated in my relationships, my images revealed my preoccupation with a sense of space. As I integrated the changes taking place in my life into a more comprehensive picture, I found my photos also concentrating on form. Now, after several months of reflection on the changes the last five years have wrought, I find myself making images of — what else? — reflections.

One of the long-standing questions I ask myself that has recently demanded an answer is *why* I photograph. For me, photography is more than a hobby, more than a job, more than an art. More than all these combined, it's a way of life, a reason for being, my life's *work* and my life's passion! It's also my way of repaying a debt and of showing my gratitude; few people have the opportunity to discover their life's dream and passion, let alone to live it. I must express my thankfulness for the gift that's been given to me.

The general atmosphere of this morning's activities provides me with another answer to this question. This morning, as on most mornings, I was hunting for my daily sustenance, much as my ancestors have done for thousands of years. But instead of shooting deer, or moose, I was seeking to shoot an *image* of a moose. I failed at that task, but found other "game" to nourish my soul and, when the pictures have been sold, to sustain my body.

The trip to the Ammonoosuc River proved to be most rewarding. As I wandered along the banks, I found numerous forms, shapes, and splashes of color reflected in the languid pools. I also found time to ponder on this morning's events. As so often happens, I set out with a set of goals that, because of uncontrollable conditions, became impossible to accomplish. Yet by remaining open and aware, I was presented with opportunities beyond my anticipation, for the wildly, breathtakingly beautiful sunrise shot is as elusive as a good moose picture! How many hours have I spent second-guessing cloud movements, selecting foreground subjects, anticipating favorable conditions when everything seemed perfect, only to have nothing happen? This morning at Pondicherry, however, I didn't think — I knew! I tingled! The sky tingled! The first blush of the eastern sky confirmed what I *knew* would happen. The longer I photograph nature and observe life, the more I learn that my intended accomplishments rarely create the best results. But if I pay attention, become sensitive to my surroundings, and truly observe, my work will often far exceed any preconceived notions of what I want.

Cobalt reflection along the Swift River.

Not being one to rest on my laurels, however, I'm off hunting moose again the next morning. Standing in the middle of what must be Grand Central Mooseway — a bog near the Swift River where literally thousands of moose feet have churned the ground to muck — I've been listening to a moose for at least ten minutes now, schlopping around somewhere nearby. He seems to move closer, then farther away. Perhaps he has caught my scent. Hours pass, but no moose. Yet this hunt is, as always, successful. Not only have I found a place where my future chances of success are significantly higher, but the delights and rewards of traveling into likely places preclude the possibility of failure.

Three months later, I'm back in this same bog. Snow lies thickly around me. Frozen ground and ice now enable me to venture into places I'd been unable to reach before. The moose tracks that crisscrossed the bog in every direction on my last visit are no longer evident; perhaps moose don't come here in winter. I'm hunting around, hoping to find even one set of fresh tracks, when I hear a sound . . . a sound like that I imagine a moose would make breaking through ice! And another sound! Different. — Back toward the road. Sounds like a semi, downshifting, upshifting, getting louder and louder. Suddenly a big bull moose crashes out from the underbrush as the truck roars by. I spin my camera sixty degrees on the tripod and get off one shot as the moose races toward me. He's just yards away, almost on top of me, before he sees me. I can almost hear him yell "Yikes!" as he spins away. My camera follows and gets a blurry image of a startled, confused moose. He crashes away back into the brush but doesn't go far, so I follow. Minutes later, I catch up with him, and we walk parallel back into the bog for about a half-mile. Then, ignoring me, he does what seems to me an incredible thing: he beds down not ten yards away, totally oblivious to my presence. Perhaps a wildlife biologist could explain this behavior, but it certainly doesn't seem that the bull perceived any danger.

I inch forward, and around. With the bull's back to me I can't get a good shot, but if I move much farther to my right brush will be in my way. When I'm only twenty feet away, he suddenly turns his great head and gives me a dirty look as if to say, "Hold it right there, buster! That's close enough." I agree, and look for a tree to climb if it should become necessary. But Mort quickly settles down (I've named the bull Morton by now), and so do I.

The rest is anticlimactic. After a while — about one roll of film — Mort gets up and starts to browse. I continue to shoot a variety of closeups, yet feel that I've already made my best image for this session. When Mort starts to slip away into the forest I thank him, apologize for any inconvenience I may have caused him, and head back for my truck. I've finally had the opportunity not only to photograph a moose, but to actually share an experience with one. Somehow, I now feel that whatever it was that I came to the White Mountains to discover, I've found it.

A myriad of colors mirrored by a thin film of water flowing over a ledge.

Two ways of photographing reflections are to include the source of reflected light (right), or to just concentrate on the reflection itself (above).

Leaves float on a small bog pond along the Zealand River (left). Clouds float on Cherry Pond just before sunrise (below).

Birches inhabit much of the same territory as moose do, are much easier to find, and don't run away.

No moose today around Red Eagle Pond (left) or Falls Pond, near Rocky Gorge on the Swift River. But ask me if I care …

Water near or at the freezing point has an interesting reflective quality different from warmer water. Sunlight reflecting off cliffs reflects again off the Ellis River (above). A skim of new ice adds texture to these pond reflections (right).

Sunlight and clouds dance on the surface of Cherry Pond. I probably became a photographer because of moments like these.

Morton takes a breather after a terrible fright. Which frightened him more, the truck or me, I'll never know.

The transition zone between bog and pond is most easily accessible in winter. Beyond the bog, larch, and spruce forests that grow along Cherry Pond lies the Presidential Range of the White Mountains.

Alan Nyiri, a seminomadic landscape photographer
based in Oneonta, New York, works throughout the
United States on projects like this book. In addition,
he creates "campus landscapes" for more than thirty
colleges and universities each year for use as color post-
cards, note cards, and prints. While he claims aspirations
no greater than "to do my work and still be able to spend
more than two months per year at home," close friends
seriously question this.

Rear cover: The Presidential Range from Pondicherry Wildlife Refuge.

ISBN 0-89272-241-x